Postcard from Nicaragua

Barry R. Ph...

viii. 87.

Postcard from Nicaragua

Steve Simpson

Ryburn Publishing

Ryburn Publishing, Halifax, England.

First published 1987.

Illustrations by Ilya Glazunov.
Reproduced by kind permission.
© Novosti Press Agency Publishing 1984

Typeset by Manor Typesetting, Bradford.
Designed by Long & Stebbens Graphic Design, Bradford.
Printed and bound in Great Britain by
Anchor Brendon Ltd, Tiptree, Essex

ISBN 1 85331 000 X

Introduction

Nicaragua suffered for forty-three years the dictatorship of the Somoza family, whose corrupt rule dragged the country and its people through rigged elections, murderous policing by the National Guard, and an economy steeped in debt to foreign lenders.

It was no surprise when a popular movement fought and finally overthrew the third Somoza in July 1979 with arms stolen from the National Guard itself. Nor was it difficult to understand why the new Sandinista government made literacy and health-care into priority programmes and kept arms in the hands of the Nicaraguan people to defend against a return of the old army leaders.

But eight years later, the Sandinistas are said to be imposing a red foothold on the mainland of the Americas, a communist threat to the national security of the United States of America.

Others maintain that the Nicaraguan people are one with their government, and are being forced into a struggle for survival and sovereignty by unjustified military attacks financed by the US.

The reality of daily life within Nicaragua has been hidden behind a storm of news items about war in Central America.

Steve Simpson is a statistician living in Bradford. He learned Spanish while living in Cuba in 1971, and has also visited Grenada and Jamaica in the Caribbean. The three letters and diary contained in this book were written while he worked in Nicaragua's statistics office and travelled in the country during three months in 1986. He took with him sports and educational material from the Tisma Project, a voluntary group in Bradford working to develop community links with the small agricultural town of Tisma. Tisma's mayor had been a member of a folk-group which visited Britain in 1985. Steve is an active member of the Tisma Project which has raised funds for a community centre and social project in the same way as have other cities in Britain that are twinned with Nicaraguan towns.

Somewhere Over The Gulf of Mexico
Monday 30 December 1985

Dear All,

It is possible that this is the only letter I'll send – it's easy to write when you're stuck in a plane for thiry hours. The only way to get from London to Managua without changing airlines is with Aeroflot, changing at Moscow then flying back over the Atlantic via Shannon and Havana. So I've been going over a day, and I'm not yet there. I didn't start off too well, leaving London on a different plane from my luggage. Someone's for the chop. Then five hours on Soviet concrete mixing with people changing to planes bound for Rome, Prague, Bangkok ... you name it, there was someone going there.

Being in Moscow seemed to bring out anti-Soviet solidarity in a lot of white people in the transit queue. Mutters of "Don't worry, I'm not going to take any pictures here. I don't want to get taken away". It was a medium wait, and the Aeroflot woman in charge of the queue seemed to sense people's feelings as she asked them to move up a little to allow the back of the queue into the waiting room: "Move this way please. I beg you to come this way ... There is nothing to be afraid of". More mutters of "Siberia". But racism finally overcame paranoia. Some Indians en route to Delhi were the first to obey the request; the fellow behind me whispered "Quick, move up, you know what these Indians are like, they'll push in anywhere". I was considering making an impromptu speech on the potential for international friendship in transit queues, but we started moving again. You should have seen the sweat on an English passenger's face when he was asked to take a bunch of keys off his belt before going through the X-ray frame.

Then through to a free meal. I sat with a Polish man, about 40, who first complained about the food on my Aeroflot flight (which he wasn't on) and then launched into a criticism of the "lack of civil rights in communist countries", especially lack of freedom to travel. Now he was off to Bangkok on his "first holiday of 1986". Shit, I thought, Nicaragua may have its own contradictions, but surely they'll be different ones.

That was confirmed straight away. Waiting for the plane to Managua, a Nicaraguan approaches two young German women with the offer of "background information on Nicaragua" to prevent shock on arrival. Other Nicaraguan men were round like flies within minutes. Then getting on the plane, I asked a Cuban whether a seat was free and I didn't understand his reply; he turned to his friend to say "This one's weak in the head", which I did understand. Do I have to return after three months? It seems an awfully short time before having to put up with this lot again.

Still, I settled down to Pluto Crime and playing with a solar-powered calculator I got for the statistical office where I'll be working. It does everything, even arithmetic with base 16, which would have been useful when Dad and I were weighing the baggage. No, hang on, there's 14lbs to a stone, 16 is for ounces and pounds, gills in a quart, bushels in an oxcart. Yes, it's going to be a real hit in Nicaragua. It might even get me into the psychiatric hospital.

Only an hour to go to Managua, probably only enough time for three meals, each one with wine. Which reminds me, I left half a flagon of unbottled wine in the cellar at home. Not to speak of a punctured tyre on the car. I can be a real arsehole sometimes.

I paid my emotional respects in Havana transit lounge, and made a phone call to my best friend there, Frency. We were cut off half-way through, and I couldn't get back to him. Luckily I'd mentioned I was only in transit, or he might have been up to meet me at the airport.

The saving grace of the journey was a really pleasant Romanian engineer who sat next to me between Moscow and Havana. He was "going to mend a vessel". We started talking after he pulled out a bagful of screwdrivers, electrical equipment, and knives. Don't Aeroflot have to be security conscious?

Arrival

The plane does a figure of eight over Managua and Managua lake. It gets very bumpy in the wind, dropping all the time and finally lands to applause from most of us on board. About 11am, Monday 30th. Straight into the queue for changing money. Non-Nicaraguans change US$60 at the low rate of 27.5 cordobas to the dollar, which gives you just enough for the taxi into Managua. It's like an airport tax, a gift to the government, because once in Managua there's an official place to change money at 750 cordobas to the dollar, over 25 times the airport rate.

Well, it's hot and Spanish-speaking (just like Cuba; this should be a doddle). All my luggage was there waiting; it must have caught up in Moscow.

But it's not like Cuba. On the way from the airport there were big adverts for La Prensa, now a religious and right-wing opposition newspaper, and for the PCN (Partido Comunista de Nicaragua), a Maoist party that's put itself in opposition to the government. Also adverts for private companies' products, for the voluntary military reserve force, for the state cultural organisation (outside a circus ring), and big billboards of Sandino and heroes of the 'Revolucion'. Private billboards advertising products just about outnumber other billboards, in Managua at least.

Check in at Hospedaje San Juan, the base for TecNICA who organise the placement of technical volunteers like me. TecNICA is run by United States citizens who are opposed to their government's policy towards Nicaragua; it has a steering group made up of Nicaraguan scientists and government officials who oversee its work. Hospedaje San Juan is a private guest house in a well-off area near the Universities, about 70p a night including food, thanks to the exchange rate. Showers, telephones ... Run by don Francisco and wife and some of their nine children. TecNICA have three people there permanently, arranging the work and visits, etc. They seem helpful. They are expecting me to start work on Monday 6th January, so I'll do my 4 weeks from then.

Managua, still Monday 30th

Took a walk to change some money. 750 cordobas to the dollar, or 730 with travellers cheques. That works out at ten a penny. It's almost giving cordobas away, but in fact is a way of keeping the black market in check. Later in the day walked into town (with a mad dog maybe) to a supermarket, about 2 miles. Met a Canadian tourist there who boasted he'd got 700 cordobas for a dollar on the black market! Pencils were 50c, oranges 8c each, a glass 380c, 1lb instant Nicaraguan coffee 70c, bottle of rum 420c, jeans 2250c, Communist Manifesto(!) 35c, a book called God Speaks Today 750c. Ten a penny remember. 80% of Nicaraguans earn 5,000 to 12,000c a month so after comparing wages the more realistic exchange is maybe nearer the airport rate – 3 pence a cordoba or thereabouts. But it's more complicated still because basic foods are distributed very cheaply on a different system so the high inflation affects most those who were used to luxuries. I'll have to find out if there's another rate for donations from abroad.

I don't think I found Managua. I got to the Hospedaje Los Santos, but there was no note from Harry Noyes. (Harry is living semi-permanently in Nicaragua. He's a friend of the first person from Bradford to visit Tisma – Kathleen Burt, who came in July 1985). Then I walked until I got lost, without finding anything that looked like a square or a major building, with the exception of the Intercontinental Hotel (good for expensive clothes and stuffed frogs at 1000c). I had been warned – Managua hasn't been rebuilt since the big earthquake in 1972 – but I was still disappointed that I couldn't find "Victory Square". Back to the hospedaje and my first tortilla – they're chapattis made out of corn – and a drink that tastes like a mixture of lemon, banana and melon; it's one fruit, grenadilla, and I want to know more about it.

I've decided to go to Tisma tomorrow, and be back here on Thursday to see the person who will be responsible for my work. Slept from 1am Bradford time until 6.30am Managua time – 11.5 hours.

Tisma, 31st December

I left at 9am carrying the volleyballs and the volleyball net, a camera and a few clothes. I don't think I could get used to carrying luggage around, but I'm trying hard. Five buses to Tisma, via Tipitapa. The first bus left me on the road out to Tipitapa, opposite El Nuevo Diario. This is the third newspaper after La Prensa and Barricada, and it's run by journalists who were booted out by La Prensa's right-wing owners for being too sympathetic to the Revolution.

The buses are something else. You squeeze in at the front, and if you're lucky you get carried slowly to the back as people get off at the back and more squeeze in at the front. That's if you're lucky. If you're unlucky you get pushed to one side and struggle continuously to prevent yourself falling on top of the people in the seats. I don't know how the people in the seats get there. They always just seem to be there and don't get off. Very experienced travellers get on last and hang on the outside of the bus with one hand. They believe it's safer than going inside.

At Tipitapa I sat down for a rest outside a barber's shop.

The barber showed me his collection of old coins – including an 1897 coin from Peru – and then told me how Nicaragua was totalitarian and that you only had to complain and you were taken off to prison. It didn't seem to square with the fact that I haven't seen a policeman yet, that he hadn't voted in the elections, and that he had a very smart barber-shop business. So I took out Jonny's Maggie Thatcher squeeze toy and told him I was a communist, and it all seemed to go down very well. Another bus to the Tisma turn-off, yet another half-way to Tisma. Well, it was a bus in the sense that everyone paid the driver but it seemed just like a lorry with an open back to me. They left me in one of Tisma district's villages, Santa Cruz, outside the house of a woman who asked me if I was Danish. During 1982-4 a brigade of Danish volunteers had built a school there. I said no, I was from Bradford, and if I was lucky I'd meet her again.

It's hot and dry; apparently Tisma didn't get it's quota of rain in 1985, and crops are well down. Finally the proper Tisma bus caught me up. They seemed to know I was coming, some of them on the bus. When one of them asked where I was from, another said I was probably going to Celso's house, which seemed to explain where I was from! (Celso visited Britain in the spring of 1985 on a gruelling international tour of a folk-group from Nicaragua's Agricultural Workers' Union. He's now mayor of Tisma).

Tisma

I can't write this like a diary since the last two days have been a continuous flood of people and information, with not much time for reflection, so I'll pick out and 'report' the bits I think I know enough about. I don't know how you managed it from cold, Kath. All your information has made it much easier to fit things in their place. I gave Isaura and family, Celso and family, and Manuel their packets from you and they're all really happy you remembered them and sent their photos and so on. To the kids I'm "Katalina's brother".

I spent the two days taking it easy and feeling comfortable, very comfortable. I've arranged with Celso to go back for the week 3rd – 9th February to work on the twinning proposal and he says he'll arrange a week of meetings with the Comite Comarcal Central – his team that has a representative from each of the 11 comarcas (rural parts surrounding the town), plus other interested people. It sounds like hard work to me; envoy Simpson began his work on 3rd February ... Celso's definitely right behind the twinning idea; he wants it to happen, and I think his expectations are not unrealistic. He doesn't talk in terms of millions of pounds, but he wouldn't object to one million! He's written a letter for the Tisma Project, which I'll enclose with this. I've left him with all the letters that were written from Bradford so he can start discussions with others before February.

Celso Chavarria Romero and Family

Nine people, three pigs and a piglet, three turkeys, one cock, two hens and four chicks, three ducks and a duckling, and me, are in a newly finished stone house on land next to the old house, a wooden shack. Celso and his family built it; it's about 25ft by 30ft, with a partition for sleeping quarters and a kitchen added on the back. The partition is breeze block from Tisma's block factory and the floor is soil that gets swept about four times a day. There are wooden rafters with tiles on top. For Tisma the conditions are good but not the best (no patio, no tiled floors, and practically no furniture except for the beds). A lot of other Tisma houses are wood, with paper to stop the draughts pasted on the outside and roofs of old thatch or patched corrugated iron. There's no electric light in this house – kerosene lamps and kerosene for cooking. No fridge – there are only four or five in Tisma, in the shops, for soft drinks and meat. No telephone – 13 telephones in Tisma. The Junta Municipal where Celso works is Tisma 04. Cesspit toilet.

The animals sleep in at night because there's no fence round their land. One thing that makes the family different – no cow. The cockerel's a bit of a pain; it crows more at night than in the day. But the pigs are really friendly and like their backs being rubbed. I never knew that about pigs.

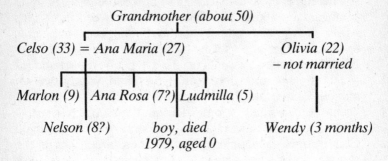

Olivia, Ana Maria's sister, is 23 on 16th January. She's one of six children, two of whom are in Tisma – Ana Maria, and another sister who lives two houses away.

At 16, after the 'Triunfo' (everybody's name for the Revolution of July 1979), Olivia was active in the Tisma CDS (Comite de Defensa Sandinista) and was offered a scholarship of four years training in Cuba as a veterinary technician. She forged her mum's signature on the first forms, knowing that her mum wanted her to have a religious career. Went to Cuba with 60 other Nicaraguan youths, and loved it – she did her final year of secondary school there, then three years of veterinary science, first in the Isla de Juventud, then in Havana.

Her group of students (Nicaraguan and Cuban) won the national emulation prize one year – a competition that mixes good grades in study, good sports, and productive manual work (she did tobacco-picking, I think). No prize, in the sense of entry to other things, but she got a medal and the group had a special fiesta laid on and really enjoyed the whole thing.

She came back to Nicaragua and has been working in Matagalpa, walking and riding horses between farms. It's within the war zone and dangerous, but nothing's happened to her yet. She enjoys it but would like a change. Comes back to Tisma every weekend she can get transport and for holidays. Her mum looks after the child Wendy who is named after a North American friend because the child "came out white"! Unmarried mothers are not at all unusual, and family planning is "only just beginning". Children get six nappies at birth – there aren't any in the shops – and that's only if the store room happens to have them in. So Wendy's got nappies made out of old clothes.

Celso

Celso's growing on me very quickly. He's gentle-strong, a bit serious and humourless, but very sensitive to other people. He's been mayor ('co-ordinador de la Junta Municipal de Reconstruccion, Tisma') since September, and seems really suited to it. It's not a political post, it's not elective and there's nothing regal about it; it's more the equivalent of 'Chief Executive' or 'Chief City Officer'. He has a staff of four who deal with some local taxes, a local budget, and co-ordination and support for all the local social and economic programmes. There's not much to co-ordinate yet, so he's more a promoter than a co-ordinator. He sees his task as mobilising people's own collective strength to solve problems that are brought to him or that he perceives.

So, for example, since September he's got together a group of 40-50 to plan and build a new 'pre-escolar', a pre-school nursery. They are mainly the director and parents of the present pre-escolar, which is cramped in a rented private building that is threatening to fall down. A site has been identified and the group is raising money locally (with donations, parties etc) to add to what they hope to get from the Ministry of Education. The pre-escalor will be built mainly by voluntary labour from within Tisma. There's another committee, of entirely different people, planning the sports area in the centre of Tisma.

There is a Comite Comarcal supported by Celso in each of the 11 comarcas (rural areas) in Tisma's district, and a Comite Comarcal Central with a representative from each of the Comites Comarcales and relevant people from Tisma town – that's what I might be attending on 3rd February. Together they represent the two to three thousand families living in the district. While I was with Celso at least ten separate individuals came to him with various problems – at home during the day, and when we were walking round the streets. One of them, for example, wanted help with writing a letter to the owner of the land he worked on.

Celso seems good at conjuring up appropriate solutions, appropriate both to the problem and to the person who has it. As a personal example, he very quickly cottoned on to the fact that I hadn't decided how and when to spend time in Tisma (well, maybe I told him!), and he suggested that I just take it easy these two days, get orientated to Tisma, then concentrate on the statistics work in Managua, and come back for a week to work at meeting Tisma people and identifying problems with him. Very obvious, very simple, and that's what I'm going to do. In fact the whole family has been warm and straight-forward – welcoming but nothing over the top. "Esta es tu casa", they said. "This is your home". Merle Collins should write a poem with that line. I feel that every town must have plenty of families like this, but I don't *believe* it.

Celso is an only child, unusual in Nicaragua, brought up by relations and then left to himself at 14. Mother in Granada now, father remarried and now in El Rama. Born and brought up in Tisma, Celso lived in Rivas (in the south west of Nicaragua) and Managua, and ended up back in Tisma. Married Ana Maria in 1973 (he was 20, she was 15), and by 1978 was working in Masaya (15km away) at odd jobs.

His first action in the war against Somoza was during the Masaya uprising in September 1978, which Celso simply "took part in", putting up barricades with friends from work, and learning to hide and escape when the National Guard came in very heavily after three days. From then he had a clandestine aerial to listen to the Sandinista radio. Some time after that he joined the Frente Sandinista de Liberacion Nacional. (That's interesting – the Sandinistas are both a very broad movement and, within that, a fairly disciplined party, requiring proof of seriousness and commitment as a pre-condition of membership). Before and after the Triunfo, Celso worked with the agricultural workers' association (ATC). He started the 'popular reporters' movement of amateur journalists sending news to the ATC paper and formed the folk group 'Heroes y Martires de San Francisco del Norte' which ended up in Bradford. He says that he's still affected by the exhaustion after that trip. He 'rested' by building the house. And so to Co-ordinador de la Junta Municipal.

It seems that Tisma district is relatively very fertile, and so it's economically quite important to Nicaragua. Most families will have little problem in getting regular food – vegetables, cornflour, milk, meat, fruit, eggs are all in Tisma, if not in each household. The area seems a bit more prosperous than what I remember of rural Grenada for instance, even if there's little commerce and no industry apart from a block factory. What Tisma lacks is organisation and finance for development.

Co-operativa Agricola Lilliam Velasquez

Lilliam Velasquez was a Tismeña who was killed in the war against Somoza. Though Tisma itself wasn't the scene of much resistance, the Guardia Civil post was burned down once. Then about 15 National Guard left when their time was up nationally; only one or two were from Tisma, I think.

I had a walk-about with Celso on Tuesday afternoon, and we came into the end of a members' meeting for this co-op. I asked them a few questions, but felt a bit embarrassed because I wasn't sure if they'd really finished their business. The co-op's been going since 1980 or 1981, with 25 members working about 120 manzanas (210 acres) of land, receiving equal wages and paying sick leave, military training leave and for one volunteer to take part in the present coffee harvest in the north of Nicaragua. They have 100 manzanas of cotton which they harvest with the help of seasonal paid labour and sell to the government buying-house, and five manzanas of tomatoes which they sell in Managua markets to private buyers who then re-sell at twice the price: a problem. Their vice-president is Dario Medina; they also have a president, treasurer and secretary. The biggest problem for this co-op is that although they could work more land, they can't get it yet.

There are over 500 families in co-ops in Tisma, some of them in the less advanced sort where the individuals keep their own land but share machinery and credit. Then there's a significant number of real peasants who own and work their own land alone; two state-owned farms; and two large privately-owned farms with waged agricultural labourers.

Then they started asking me questions. What was grown in Bradford? (Herbs?) Did I come by boat or by aeroplane? Which party did I represent? (The Tisma Project Party. But later I let on that I had some personal characteristics too). Did I like Margaret Thatcher? What will happen when Margaret Thatcher goes? Didn't I have any training with arms? And they weren't embarrassed at all asking questions.

They had a load of irrigation piping stacked up, ready to be put in place this spring. Maybe there's a project there with another co-op.

La Poza

On New Years Day I went with Isaura, Julio and family (Kath ate with them in the summer) to the local beauty spot – la Poza, a spring that's filled a hollow to make a lake about 100 yards across. There were about 150 people of all ages there, picnicking and swimming in filthy water (it's usually a watering-place for cattle). I joined in with everyone else – once you forget that the water is black with mud from the bottom, it's refreshing. I only saw about half a dozen people swimming (rather than playing in the water).

Another of Celso's ideas is to make this into a proper recreation area. He wasn't there – he doesn't smoke, drink, go to fiestas, or picnic; I forgot to say that before. Quote of the day came from a passer-by who, on learning that I was from Gran Bretana, said "Una vez acabada con la agresion aqui, cogeremos a Margaret Thatcher, pondremos piedras en las pies, y vamos a meterle en la poza esta", i.e. "Once we've finished with the aggression here, we'll get hold of Margaret Thatcher, tie stones to her feet, and throw her in la Poza".

Doctor, doctor

No doctor comes now. The clinic has four nurses and the nearest doctor is in Masaya. (On the bus I took to Masaya there were four kids who all looked ill. Ana Maria's fourth child died because she couldn't get him to Masaya). Celso assures me that if foreign doctors were to come to Tisma, they would get all the assistance that the Ministry of Health can give. There are few doctors in Nicaragua, except those at the war zone.

Adult Education

Adolfo Somethingo, 'promoter' of adult education for Northern Tisma, responsible for five maestros populares in his area, also for adult education in the Balsamo farm, where he works full-time. I'll see him again.

Schools

Are on holiday January and February (harvest time). But the teachers are about. Celso suggests twinning Carlton Bolling Upper School in Bradford with La Escuela del Norte, which has pupils at 13 and above. More schools in Bradford, more schools in Tisma. Seems sensible. I might just catch the new term at the beginning of March.

That's Tisma for now. Celso sees the Bradford link as important because it's continuous contact. Tisma benefited from a donation of 3 million cordobas from a town in West Germany that's twinned with the Masaya region but there was no follow-up. It seems like the project can be a real help to Tisma and Nicaragua.

Masaya

Notice in a corner shop: "Atencion. Damos masajes – comidas vegeterianias – quiropractico – curamos enfermedades de toda clase con vegetales. Lugar: casa Hogar Naturista, 'Koinonia', Km 17 Carretera Managua – Masaya. Consulta: Domingo a jueves de 8 a 5pm". ("Attention, we give massage – vegetarian food – chiropractor – we cure illnesses of all kinds with vegetables. [Address and times]). The shop had granola on sale in a special cabinet; the owner didn't know anything about it – seemed a bit amused and hadn't seen the supplier for months. "It doesn't sell very well".

Money – donations

I'm getting an idea of what and how to send, but not a very clear one. The rate for donations is officially 100 cordobas to the dollar. It's OK to change dollars at the 750 rate tourists get and to hand over the money, but only $100 at a time. Tisma needs money as much as it needs goods, because a lot of basic stuff, including building material, *is* available at a price. Technical stuff and things that have to be imported are definitely best sent as material, not money; and pencils, paper, etc, are not *un*wanted at all.

To get things out:

a) NSC (Nicaragua Solidarity Campaign) brigadistas are all asked to leave 2 kilos of space for taking material – which can include Tisma Project material. Address to Dave Thompson, NSC rep in Nicaragua, who meets all the brigadistas. Write to him in advance with details of exactly what to expect, and what it's for in Tisma. Also, write to Celso and tell him to expect it.

b) Containers: package and label to Dave Thompson and write to him as above. He'll make sure it gets to Tisma. He'll get and send us a receipt. The next container from NSC may be for the Ministry of Education – DT knows them well and they would pass on anything addressed to him.

c) Money more than $100 should go officially through FACS – the organisation here that deals with all overseas donations of money. I don't know the details of this. I'll find out.

There's the Oficina de Hermamiento – I'll go there in the next couple of weeks. It's the twinning office.

There's someone going to the USA tomorrow morning so now I'm rushing to finish this tonight so that he can post it from there and save two or three weeks in the mail.

I saw my bosses at the Statistics and Census Office today. It's a massive place. The person responsible for my work struck me as a worried slob, but I only had half an hour with him today (Friday January 3rd). I start on Monday, assessing their sampling frames for agriculture and houses – the list of areas/farms and houses which they use to take surveys from, but which they know is out of date. It's not what I thought I was going to do, and I know sod-all about it – they picked it up from part of my CV which says I looked at health service sampling frames as part of an MSc course in 1978. I did? Oh well, I don't think they expect much, so we agree on that. They've got a good library, so maybe I can learn about it for a week and let them tell me about it for three weeks. If they've time. In emergency you can telephone me at the hospedaje, but I may not be here. 7am breakfast (no porridge), 1pm your time.

POR LA PAZ, TODOS CONTRA LA AGRESION,

Con saludos sandinistas,

El Chele (the white man)

26 January, 1986
"1986: AFTER 25 YEARS, EVERY EFFORT AGAINST THE AGGRESSION"
(This appears on letters from any government office. The FSLN was founded 25 years ago. So I'm not a government office? What the hell).

Casares, on the Pacific coast.

Dear All,
Let me talk you through this scene. The sand is hot. 50 yards away the surf is breaking over a dozen people lying in the water. Over to the left, another fishing boat has just been pulled up the beach to join the twenty or so already there. Above the boats, the wooden Hotel Casino is blasting out a mixture of Beatles and Nicaraguan juke-box records. I'm in the beach cafe next door under a tree shade, drinking with three buddies from the TecNICA group at a rough wooden table, writing to you. We arrived in a taxi. The

Nicaraguan family at the next table are drinking rum. They're probably on holiday. The one-ton pig under the tree told me she lives here. This is the Pacific. I came here two weeks ago, too, for a weekend break.

I got a call last week from the Intercontinental Hotel, from Joss who had just arrived from Leeds and beat the four-week post – so I got a packet of things from Kath, Jonny, and a second letter from Mum and Dad. That was a really thoughtful touch, Jonny – to include a couple of circulars and a bill so I wouldn't get homesick. Joss is going back on Thursday, so if he's got some space I'll get this letter to him, and some books I've bought for the Tisma Project bookstall. It was such a surprise getting all that post – he's a friend for life, whether he likes it or not. And since there's so much going on in Bradford, I can see there's not much need for me there. So maybe I'll stay here for a couple of years.

I've been here nearly four weeks, and I still feel very comfortable. The rest of January's TecNICA group arrived from the USA, and most of them left again yesterday. I've been full time at the statistics institute, at TecNICA meetings and visits in the evenings, a group trip up to Matagalpa and Jinotega in the north last weekend, and now some relaxing and drinking this weekend.

It may be boring, but I'm going to tell you about some of those things. First, the work. I spent most of the first two weeks giving myself a conversion course to agricultural survey work and understanding what they do here in Nicaragua. The worried slob who is officially in charge of me passed me straight on to the head of the 6-person cartography department. His name is – wait for it – Noel Leon. His parents must have enjoyed making that one up.

The annual survey they have done is directed towards knowing the production of maize and beans. Since Nicaragua is only planning to survive during the next couple of years, and since maize and beans are the staple foodstuffs (maize to make tortillas), it's essential to know how much is being grown in order to plan how much foreign currency is going to be needed for imports. And unlike coffee, sugar or rice, both maize and beans are mainly cultivated by individual campesinos or small co-ops, so going out and asking every producer is out of the question. Therefore a well-designed survey of a sample of manageable-sized areas gives the information. 'Manageable-sized' is what an interviewer/field worker can manage in a day, about one square kilometre.

The cartography department has maps of Nicaragua covered in lines that divide the country up into areas from which the survey takes samples. To make the sample a bit less haphazard than a complete random sample, each little area is also marked with the results of a census from a few years ago, so the survey can be made more representative by including different kinds of area – at least, areas that were different from each other at the time of the census a few years ago. That's the theory. In practice the survey had to be discontinued last summer because the contras were in the north and south; some areas couldn't be entered from time to time, and three Land-Rovers used by survey workers were snatched or destroyed in the north. At the same time there are doubts about the census information. In fact this didn't come from a census at all, but from meetings of Agricultural Reform workers in each area, many of whom hadn't been working in their area very long. And finally, the Agrarian Reform Ministry (MIDINRA) doesn't trust surveys and wants to do its own thing, but it isn't sure what or how. (MIDINRA is the most powerful ministry in Nicaragua because so many resources are going into improving agricultural production, and it has a lot of popular support for its programmes, unlike INEC, the survey and census institute.

That's what I understood after two weeks. Their question had been "Look this over, maybe you can come up with a few ideas about INEC's surveys". Last week I'd identified a couple of things I could do to sort out how good or bad that 'census' information is for basing the survey on, when on Friday – no, Thursday – it was announced that every INEC programme would close down for a month and a half, so that anyone willing could go out and help bring in the coffee harvest!

That's how things are. I'll see what I can do next week, and maybe come back for a couple of days before leaving Nicaragua. That's how things are; moving from one crisis campaign to the next. Coffee gets a good price on the international market right now, so every sackful helps get foreign currency, which in turn helps beat the US trade embargo: helps, for instance, to replace those three INEC Land-Rovers. As it was put at the INEC meeting that called for coffee harvest volunteers, "We do not say that we are closing INEC to bring in the coffee harvest – we are going to bring in the coffee so that INEC may stay open". That's how things are.

People who I'm directly working with are great. Noel is a Frente member, one of the few really committed-to-the-country professional workers I've met. The others in the cartography department are much like any other office workers. Larry is from the Atlantic coast and is bilingual. Occasionally we talk English, but he is a bit embarrassed about it because he has been in Managua 8 years and hasn't spoken English much in that time – I have a feeling too that he regards his Caribbean English as somehow inferior to my standard (!) English.

I think they are all, like most people, 'with the Revolution' in the sense that the last thing they'd want is victory for the contras, but none of them seem to be involved in any big way except for Noel. In another office where I've got a desk there are five women and the only one who thinks and talks politics is an Argentinian, Miri, who since having to leave her country has been in Sweden, Cuba and now Nicaragua. Generally, foreigners here are left-wing – that's usually why they are here after all.

One of the Nicaraguans here makes a big joke out of

marrying me and going to England, seeing London (no interest in Bradford), wearing fur coats and living a life of luxury. I can't put her off with stories of snow and rain or unemployment. That's not to say they don't know what their problems are. They talk all the time about things that are difficult to get hold of, about crowded transport, about people charging high prices for imported goods, though they do a bit of that themselves – someone will have a relative who has brought fancy clothes from Costa Rica and they'll bring it into work to sell. The story goes that one make-up set from abroad came into INEC and was sold in the morning for 2000 cordobas. It was resold six times and finally left INEC with someone who parted with 4000 cordobas for it.

Work discipline is pretty low at INEC – plenty of loafing about. After all, the workers are in control now, so those who aren't particularly socially conscious take advantage of the fact that they're not likely to be sacked by a wicked employer. The opportunities for training and being promoted are here in abundance, but the financial rewards aren't so very great, so again those who 'respect their work' and are socially conscious are most likely to get promoted. That's great, up to the point that work doesn't get done because there aren't enough socially conscious people around. For example, in the cartography department, Fatima types for an hour and sleeps the rest of th day, or goes out and does her shopping. It may be partly that the suspension of the agricultural survey means that she hasn't got so much work to do; but at the same time there are plenty of courses she could be doing and no-one would object to her studying at work. But she doesn't want to.

Alongside continuous campaigns and propaganda encouraging people to become socially conscious – education campaigns, coffee harvest appeals, etc, there's now a wage structure that's supposed to give incentives to 'get on' and get promoted. It goes by the fine name of SNOTS and operates in all state-financed jobs, negotiated at national level between government and unions.

Working hours are 8 – 12, 1 – 5.30, Mon – Sat. So I've learnt I can get up before 7am every day. It's easy really. First you have to go to bed at 10 every night. And then you have to make sure everyone else does as well so as not to feel you're missing out on anything. That's how I see it anyway.

Food at work is fine. Meat every day. Hard on vegetarians, though. It's usually meat and beans and rice and plantains and refresco – fresh juice with the fruit of the day. Two really offensive things about the food arrangements, however. Firstly the queue. People arrive and walk along the queue looking for someone they know at the front. So if you don't do that it doesn't matter when you arrive; you still end up at the back of the queue. There ought to be a better union here!

The second thing that really offends me is: no puddings. No custard, no tarts, no sponge, not even rice pudding. It really takes the edge off a country when you have to walk the streets looking for someone to sell you a piece of cake. But that's what I do. I've been told that the Hotel Intercontinental has a cheap buffet lunch that includes a free choice of as many puddings as you want. The first day I'm in Managua and not working ... the first day I'm in ...

Sorry, I was dreaming. So that's work. What else do you want to know about?

Well, there's the TecNICA group. I've never met such a number of attractive North Americans in one place at the same time. By 'attractive' I mean friendly, interesting, committed, fun, and they don't act as though they know all about you before you open your mouth. Some of them are full of shit, but that's due to stomach troubles (which I've been free of so far. If I'm full of shit it's for real).

The number of US citizens here must be an influence against an invasion. Allen Ginsberg is here now. Bob Dylan due later in the year. Sometimes it gets a bit much. For example: there's a demonstration each Thursday morning outside the US embassy in Managua. I went the second

Thursday here. They were almost all US citizens it seemed to me, so I scribbled out a notice saying "UK says peace" and proudly held it up on the edge of the crowd of about 100 people. Maybe I should have put "England" or "Britain", but "UK" is much shorter to write out. After it was over (about half an hour of speeches from different brigades who were here, and a person from the peace march through Central America who hadn't been allowed into Honduras), someone comes over to me and says ... "Say, you from the University of Kentucky too?"

About half of the TecNICA people are computer technicians who come for two weeks to fix computers, write programs, or teach courses, mainly in the ministries. But on this group there are also a mechanic, a machinist, a chemist, and a seismologist. The mechanic and the chemist are Boris and Julie, brought up together in the Bronx, New York, on a big housing co-op in the thirties and very involved in the progressive movement up to the late forties or early fifties, including the Communist Party. Boris drove the lead bus out of a big Paul Robeson open-air concert through a gauntlet of Ku Klux Klan stones. Julie's staying on an extra week because he's enjoying it so much here. He's convinced me that if it wasn't so difficult and expensive to arrange, I would definitely go back via the US.

TecNICA is a really good way of getting to know Nicaragua. The placements are a bit haphazard, and so the work that gets done varies a lot from person to person. But that doesn't seem to matter to the Nicaraguans – I guess anything that gets done is a good result. After all it's voluntary and doesn't cost Nicaragua a cordoba. Most evenings we've had people visiting or trips out, and last weekend we went north. I'm not sure how much to report. I'll pick out a few things.

One night we had Anibal Zuniga, 25 years old, who works in the Foreign Ministry on US affairs. A lot of the talk and questions were on the contras and the internal opposition, and a lot of what he said is backed up by what I read in the newspapers. This is what he said to us.

The government is quite certain that in 1985 the contras and the US aims were defeated strategically. The contras had been financed to seize and occupy a small part of Nicaragua, anywhere, proclaim a government parallel to the real government, and then under international law they would be able to call on other countries' governmental assistance, including the US marines. That strategy is now definitely defeated, militarily: the contras no longer have a chance of doing it.

In a sense this means that the threat of a direct US invasion is more on the cards, without any reference to international law, because this would be the only way left of bringing down the government from outside, but what's happening is that in three ways the contras and the US are trying other strategies before committing themselves to a direct invasion:

First the contras are infiltrating groups into Nicaragua to commit sabotage and terrorist acts. Schools near the border with Honduras have been burnt down. Last week an electricity pylon in the north was blown up. "They have no choice but to try to terrorise the people – because they have absolutely nothing to offer them".

Secondly, they have been trying to raise the technical level of the war against Nicaragua. For instance, Nicaraguan helicopters patrolling the border with Costa Rica were fired at from inside Costa Rica earlier in January; it is likely that the ex-National Guard on the Honduran border will get rockets to fire from Honduras; and apparently there's even been talk of supplying the contras with aeroplanes.

And thirdly, that part of the opposition within Nicaragua which hasn't accepted that the government is legitimate – for example, parties that refused to register and contest the 1984 election, and the La Prensa newspaper – have become more active, and talk publicly of unity with the contras, with the contras as their military arm. That and the new contra strategy of sabotage, 'an internal front', was what prompted the State of Emergency in autumn 1985.

Because of the amount of money channelled through the

CIA, and the evidence of training contras in Honduras, the Nicaraguan government feels that the US administration is organising and activating these new tactics directly. The fear is a 'war of attrition', preventing the social programmes going ahead, creating discontent that things aren't improving materially in Nicaragua, combined with a campaign of lies in the international sphere to isolate the government from active support. 60% of the 1986 budget is for defence.

"But they should know that when a mother has three children in the military reserve, and one has been killed by the contras, and a relative has been raped by them, that family may complain about life, may even wish that this government would go, but they will never welcome the contras. The US should know that the Nicaragua they face is not an army, but a people in arms". However, they can *imagine* a situation so desperate because of this war of attrition, a future lack of food for example, that the US could see an opportunity to come in as saviours.

Ciudad Sandino

The area of this Managua 'suburb' we visited has a hundred or so families who organised themselves to move from the central Managua earthquake ruins where they had been squatting. A Swiss agency pays for most of the materials, but all the labour to put up houses came from the inhabitants while they were still living in the old ruins: 420 hours' labour plus 25 cordobas a week to pay transport costs for the materials entitles a family to move in – not necessarily into the same house they helped to build since it's a collective project and the 420 hours might be spent on several different houses.

Winkler Anderson showed us round; he's one of the organisers who had lived in the ruins for 9 years. The name is from the Atlantic coast community, originally brought as slaves by temporary British colonisers, where English is still the first language. 70% of the labour on the housing project has been done by women – "the men are more often drunk". They share what skills they have and get very little help from government ministries except the original land titles. That's interesting – the land is held not by the collective, nor by the government, but by the youngest child in the family, so it cannot be sold until that child gets of legal age.

They've not got electricity yet. They used to get a line from a neighbour who had been living in the new place before, but when she demanded that they give her one of the new plots of land (because they're bigger), they refused (because the ruins' squatters had priority) and she cut off their electricity.

They've just finished a communal building which will double as a school. Winkler was asked to join the FSLN, but "I'm not ready yet. Maybe in two years. I want to put all my effort into finishing this project". He's an only child. Maybe there's something in that – some only children make the Revolution their family.

There's a lot of new fairly basic settlements in Managua – mainly of people from outside the city. It's said that Managua is the fastest growing city in Central America, but no-one knows how many live there (that's right, the 1982 census was cancelled due to lack of resources, and the contras). It's probably about 750,000 of Nicaragua's three million population. Families displaced by the contra attacks in the north move in to look for work or often hope to earn a living as street sellers – more on that later.

The Silva Negra Hotel, Matagalpa

Silva Negra means black forest. It was built by Germans after the second World War in an area that does look just like the Black Forest. We stayed there last weekend on our trip out, and got drunk, just like everyone else.

Resettlement Camp, Loma Alta Co-op

On Sunday, we went up to the north of Jinotega, an area where there has been a lot of contra activity. No checks on us at all, but we went with a regional official who had checked that it seemed safe that day.

Loma Alta is an agricultural co-op made up of two dozen families who had to move down from even further north. We piled out of the minibus and talked to the first person we met. He'd been attacked five times in the place he'd been, and was happy to be less isolated. The co-op grows coffee now, but wants more land with soil suitable for growing maize and beans for member families, and has high hopes from the latest round of agrarian reform.

As we were talking, two uniformed kids with rifles came past – they're part of the co-op and enrolled in the military reserve too. Ages: 14 & 15. On the shack nearest the road, a sign said: "Prices of transport from Loma Alta: 40c, etc. ... if any driver asks for more, report it to the FSLN. Death to the profiteers". I think the use of the word 'death' might have been a bit of a joke, but the profiteering is serious.

In Matagalpa, we talked to a group of women who had lost children and/or husbands to the Guardia. There, and at the co-op, they never used the word 'contra' like they do in Managua. It was always the 'Guardia', the National Guard of Somoza who make up most of the leadership of the contras. It was a very difficult meeting for everyone present. One by one, seventeen recounted their history. Each had lost a member of her family, sometimes more than one.

"My husband left for work one day and didn't come back. He was murdered by the Guardia. I have a son who was murdered too because he was defending us; his name is Juan; he was a mechanic. I have three other children mobilised and I am afraid that the same will happen to them".

"My son fell in Rio Coco, in Northern Zelaya, four years ago, killed by Somozist Guardia, along with twelve others. Their bodies were never recovered".

"My son Jose Rodriguez was 17 years old when the Guardia murdered him. They took his eyes out, they gouged them out then mutilated him in other ways ..." (a long pause while she gained her strength again), "Why does Reagan do this? He cannot have come from the body of a mother. It doesn't matter to us that we have to live poorly, just eating beans, but we just want to live in peace".

"I am nervous. It does me harm to talk about it. He fell six months ago. We want to ask God that our children will be safe and we will live in peace".

"I don't have the strength or bravery to talk about it ..." (another murmurs "she lost her daughter"), "I have other children. I live in constant fear as more corpses are brought in".

So what's in the papers, I can hear you asking.

Local News

The two big stories at the beginning of January were about the profiteers and the reform of the Agrarian Reform.

Profiteers

To be able to pay for the defence of Nicaragua, the government has had to print more money – for clothes, food, salaries, and so on. That means more money around than goods to buy, and that means retailers put their prices up – inflation. No-one has seen official figures, but a TecNICA economist who's been here a while reckons it was about 400% in 1985. It has weird effects – government producers and shops don't take advantage of the situation, and so can't pay their workers as much as private companies who exploit the situation fully. But the profiteers aren't big businesses – these are very closely watched – but thousands of small middle-men and street-sellers who push up prices of clothes, food, household goods – anything.

The ENABAS (government-financed) shops sell basic goods very cheaply, which means no-one goes completely short, but in a way they also fuel the inflation because there's more money left circulating for the profiteers. On January 1st the wages in all state institutions and industries were more-or-less doubled. It had happened during 1985 too, but this time the wage rise was accompanied by a press and TV campaign against the profiteers, organising the market stall-holders who were prepared not to raise prices (the campaign says the wholesalers are the worst offenders), whilst the CDS (Comites de Defensa Sandinista, on each block) have appointed 'popular inspectors' to report those retailers who raise prices a lot to the papers or to the FSLN, and generally make things difficult for profiteers.

Every day there have been articles in Barricada and El Nuevo Diario exposing profiteers, applauding the small market stall-holders, and explaining how the whole thing works. Irene, the office workers' union official who was in Britain last November (I saw her for an hour a couple of weeks ago, and arranged to go back later – she's just the same bundle of brightness) said profiteering was a big problem because thousands of families depend on street-sellers who have been keeping their income up through selling at high prices. And I don't see how the campaign can solve it in the long run. There will still be a lot of money chasing more goods than are available. Irene's answer was "produce more" – i.e. through increased productivity there would be more goods to buy to soak up the excess money. So in Nicaragua high productivity is directly in workers' interests?

Reform of the Agrarian Reform

In the new year, all lower limits to the confiscation of land holdings were dropped. Any land that is idle because the owner isn't willing to cultivate or use it can now be handed over to campesinos who are willing to use it, without compensation. There was a big send-off to the reform with campesinos in the north given land titles along with guns to defend their new land from contras.

So what's good about hundreds and thousands of individual private landowners? It's a turnaround from 1984 when the land reform had all but stopped, and resources were being put into large scale agricultural development. From what I can make out, 1986 is the (first) year of survival. No money for big projects. Whoever is willing to produce on the land should be able to do so.

The drift of landless campesinos into the towns, squatting and street-selling, and the pressure for land from those who have had to move out of the contra areas, make sense of the reform – the backbone of the revolutionary movement has been and needs to be the rural workers. Co-ops are right-on, but food is the main thing, whoever produces it. So Barricada reports rural workers holding meetings and demanding land to work on and really encourages it. (Maybe there is unused land in Tisma – but I have a feeling that the region is well cultivated already). Did I say: Barricada is the daily FSLN newspaper which also gives the fullest reporting of government initiatives. El Nuevo Diario is independent, critical, but definitely supportive of the Revolution and its progress. La Prensa is right-wing religious, trying to hold on to its past prestige, and has contra links.

Other Nicaragua news

Big campaign against doctors who don't put in many hours (apparently it's not quite true that there are very few doctors in Nicaragua; there are very few good ones), combined with attacks on private doctors.

There've been over 100 cases of malaria in Tipitapa – 20km from Tisma.

The coffee harvest is big news. And today 80 people from INEC left for a month. It's the fourth year that a general call has gone out for volunteers. Rosa-Maria from the office in which I have a desk: "Yes I'm going. I've been to the first three, so how am I going to miss this one?" There seems to be a lot of support for the idea of helping to bring in the coffee. Everyone I've spoken to who hasn't gone had a reason why they couldn't go – no-one's said they wouldn't *want* to go.

International news

Not as much as I'm used to! There's been a bit about "Thatcher's Westlandgate", but nothing juicy. Are there Heseltine and Brittan defence committees? I think there should be. And if Thatcher gets booted out, a Thatcher defence committee. Anything to make them fight each other. The Cuban Prensa Latina agency picked up an article in the Morning Star by Karl Dallas about the CIA and drugs trafficking, and it got reported here as "Karl Dallas, an expert, exposed ... etc". I'm sure he was the folk music critic up until December! A couple of weeks ago there was a paragraph about two more women being arrested at Greenham.

Talking about inflation, I think I mentioned that when we went to the beach we took a taxi – about 80km there and 80km back. It was 20,000 cordobas between four of us. That's more than most people earn in a month. If you read some of this and wonder what's going on – is Nicaragua socialist or isn't it – I'm trying to work that one out as well. The FSLN are very good at not answering that question – they're determined that support for Nicaragua should not be on the basis of ideological affiliations, but because of Nicaragua's right to do what it wants and their confidence that the practical social programmes deserve support.

Next to my work-place at INEC is the Linda Vista

cinema. Last week they were showing 'Maniobras en la cama' – 'Manouevres in bed'. This week it's 'Angel', more soft porn.

Joss leaves for England on Thursday, and I'm going to see if he has any space in his luggage. If so, I'll give him a pile of cards, books, and diaries if I can get them, for the Tisma Project stall.

Last week I went to the National Twinning Office in Nicaragua and had a cup of coffee with Francisco Valladares. He was all for laying on transport for the whole of next week in Tisma, but I refused since Celso doesn't even have a motorbike and it seemed unjustified. Maybe I was wrong. Anyway, Francisco was squaring it all with the Masaya (region 4) government office, and I may get a lift to Tisma on Monday with all the sellotape/pencils/tape measures. Good old Francisco.

I've just discovered that I've lost the address to which money from the Tisma Project should be sent. It's been one of those days today. Losing that address doesn't seem surprising. I put in 2000 data to the computer yesterday, and 'verified' them today by typing them in again. Then I discovered something was wrong with the disk, so I had to type them all in again from the start, and verify them again! I'm a dab hand at touch-typing numbers now.

To end on a high note: food. But first the bad news – turtle eggs. Don't ever ask for them. I didn't. I thought I was getting an omelette. Now the good news – zapote. It's called mamey in Cuba and elsewhere. It's a mango with the texture of an avocado pear. And remember the 800c buffet lunch at the Intercontinental? I do, I'm getting taken there tomorrow by people at work. So much for work discipline, I can't imagine we'll be there for less than two hours.

Lots of love

Esteban

Letter No. 3

Hospedaje San Juan
MANAGUA
NICARAGUA LIBRE
Sunday February 16th 1986

Dear All

The Hospedaje is quiet today. The February group has gone to Lake Jiloa to swim and sun themselves. I've moved in with Ed, a long term volunteer economist, since his room-mate Mirna had to return to the USA because her grandmother died. That is sad – she was very close to her.

I've asked Aeroflot to confirm a return flight on March 10th, and although it's three weeks away I feel very much as if I'm winding down my stay here. But I might still fit in a week on the Atlantic coast, a visit to Leon to the north of Managua, and a few more days in Tisma; and in Managua I need to sort out the need for other statistician volunteers to come. Nonetheless, it feels as though those things are filling out and rounding off the trip ...

The first week in February, 3rd – 9th, was Tisma week, and rewwarding in every way. We've got projects set up, some with budgets, biographies, maps, letters from school children and the health centre, and a ton of slides. I sat in on the first women's meeting for a year, a general assembly in one of the rural comarcas, a couple of Celso's chats in Tisma and another comarca, and I've notes on the schools, health centre, co-ops, bank, library, and a dairy farm. You're going to have to think of how to get it all out of me in Bradford!

And there's plenty I didn't find out. It's definitely on for as many people as possible to come out, for a day or two out of a general Nicaragua trip, or for longer. The only problem would be Spanish – Juanita the librarian is the only person I've met in Tisma who speaks some English. Celso and Ana-Maria want to put up anyone who comes – they're already talking about adding a partition to make a visitors' room. I said that isn't necessary; the people visiting would want to live as they do. But I suspect they won't be deterred.

I've found Tisma really exciting in the sense that it could really make use of the kind of support we could give, and it's self-contained in a way that makes it easier to understand and follow its development.

Tisma is not on the way to any other town; its size is such that most people know of each other and Tisma-led social programmes have a direct effect for most Tisma people. It lacks money above all else, and the medium-sized support that Bradford might be able to provide will have an immediate use. It was not very involved in the overthrow of Somoza, so a lot of people are indifferent to participating in the new organisations and possibilities that the revolution offers, but Celso seems to be changing that rapidly by setting up new forums where nitty-gritty problems can be expressed, and then pointing out and explaining how they can be solved with some working together on community projects, help from himself, the council and ministries, and making use of internationalist support.

I missed a 'Cara al Pueblo' – 'Face the People' – meeting on February 1st in Tisma. This was one of the weekly regional Face the People meetings, held each time in a different town. The regional representatives of each ministry literally face a meeting to which everyone in Tisma has been invited (well, there were some complaints from comarcas about not receiving invitations), and anyone can present problems and expect an immediate reply. Celso had done the ground work of getting people in each area of Tisma together to discuss what were the real problems to sort out and get an answer to.

Among the results: Tisma council's first bus arrived a week later, with the promise of 3 or 4 more. It'll go direct the 45 km to Managua, where many people living in Tisma work (also ideal for visiting twinners ...) 3 times a day for 30 cordobas. A visiting doctor 2 days a week; water to one of the comarcas which had none – it had to have water carried in lorries; and the Ministry of Construction has started to deepen a water course which last year during the rainy season was so silted up that it flooded and destroyed nearby crops. These Face the People meetings are an extra way of getting Ministry priorities sorted out. They cut out a lot of the bureaucracy – and travel – of getting the local council to make written requests to a Ministry office in another town.

These are the projects that Celso has sorted out for us to support, in his order of priority and mostly discussed with other members of the Tisma committee – the Comite Comarcal Central. The first one is a project that has been much discussed already in Tisma, and a group of people are willing to get on with it as soon as they have the money to buy materials. If we have specific ideas of projects that we can better support, then the next person to come can follow them up – some of these are ones I pushed because they seemed either manageable in the short-term, or they would be well understood in Bradford.

1. SPORTS DEVELOPMENT

a) All materials for a CHILDREN'S AND SPORTS PARK in the main Tisma square – enclosing wall, soft drinks stall, concrete volleyball/basketball ground, swings, seats, plants.
BUDGET: 715,000 cords.

b) Enclosure of the BASEBALL GROUND in the north of Tisma town, with wire fencing-materials.
BUDGET: 452,200 cords.

Most of the voluntary labour to get these done is organised by Tisma's baseball team, El Bionico – they're another tale to tell.

2. *Rebuilding of the 'CASA DE CULTURA'*
– the cultural centre. All materials.
BUDGET (provisional): 500,000 cords.

3. *MUSICAL GROUPS*
For a Tisma group sponsored by Tisma Council.
3 Guitars
Maracas   available in Nicaragua.
Xylophone   *BUDGET (provisional): 300,000 cords.*
Bongos
Piano Accordion   – NOT available in Nicaragua.
BUDGET: needs pricing in London.

4. *CARPENTRY TOOLS*
For a Tisma Council-sponsored workshop for training and use by co-operatives. Celso is working on a list and a budget for what's available in Nicaragua.

5. *BICYCLE PLUS HELMET*
For use by Tisma Council. Celso is getting prices – they're available here.

6. *EXERCISE BOOKS, PENCILS, CRAYONS*
Are always welcome for the primary school but we didn't make it a specific project. They are sometimes available in Nicaragua (I just got hold of 60 exercise books at 10 cords each in Managua, but they were supposed to sell only 10 to each customer, because of shortages). Particularly for the rural comarca schools.

7. HEALTH AND SECONDARY SCHOOLING

I've got letters to Shipley Health Centre for Maggie and Les, and to Judy for the Community Health Group, and letters to pupils in Carlton Bolling School, and a list of needs for the Health Centre and the Tisma Secondary School. Both Celso and I thought it better to have these projects specifically for health and school groups to work on directly, and separately from the other projects which would be Tisma Project collective responsibilities. What do you think?

I was keen to find some project which was directly related to agriculture and the co-ops in Tisma, but we couldn't come up with anything beyond the carpentry workshop. The irrigation and equipment is available through low-interest loans to the co-ops, and concentration on just one co-op to help doesn't seem suitable. Celso and other people here have the idea of developing the secondary school – which at present stops at 9th grade (age about 14) – into an agricultural college, but this isn't much more than idea. Anyway, I've left Celso with our commitment to support anything in that direction, and I've got a lot of information on the agricultural co-ops.

The other area I said we'd be keen to support was women's organisation. Their major problem, the one they talked about most at the women's meeting (about 30 present), was lack of work. A bad cotton harvest this year, and switching from cotton to maize and beans means little seasonal harvest work. And the clamp-down on high-priced unregistered market sellers means Tisma women can't sell family fruit and veg in Masaya as easily as before. Their favoured option is a clothes-making factory, but there's no clothing material and I had to say that I didn't think we could ensure a regular supply of cloth from Britain. Any ideas?

I bet there are loads of other projects that would be easy to feed into, adult education for instance. And although the health needs and basic educational materials will go partly to the comarcas, I didn't get a grip on how to keep the comarcas on an equal footing with the town. Maybe that's partly due to the comarcas themselves being less organised than the town, but there must be ways of giving them a bigger part of the support we can mobilise. Another longer term project, or maybe shorter term, is to fund or buy automatic machinery for the block making plant – the person who runs it says it doesn't supply the demand within Tisma even when it's working flat out.

Finally (maybe) on projects, Tisma gets some internationalist support from elsewhere. A West German project for Masaya Department as a whole gave 3 million cordobas for construction which will be used to build the new Nursery school in Tisma town; it doesn't include teaching materials but Celso hopes they'll follow up with that, so he doesn't think we should put this as a priority yet. Leicester may be supporting a housing project as part of their support for Masaya region. And Danish brigades built 5 schools in Tisma's comarcas between 1981 and 1984 with Danish government money. There are 4 Danish people here now doing improvements to these schools, but no wider follow up nor other projects. So while Tisma will use whatever it is offered, the idea of a more-or-less permanent link that can respond to needs as they arise seemed appreciated.

I took maps of Britain that show Bradford as the capital,

and a few of the photos taken at John's Tisma party in December. I've put them up in (a) the post office, (b) the council office, and (c) the agricultural bank, as these are the most-visited places!

Nidia, another of Ana-Maria's sisters who's now living in their house, took a fancy to Jonny's eyes and told me to say so. She and Ana-Maria are a laugh: "So I went to Managua to spend Christmas with my mother, and of course I took a pig with me for us to eat. In the bus and all, and following me down the street to her house. You can imagine, it was hard to kill it. I was tearful. And so was the pig, because you see it knew me. Poor little pig. But of course after I killed it, it forgot about me completely. You see? That's how it is!" And Nidia tells some yarns about local witches, and others about widows and corn-cobs.

Kath's friend Harry came to Tisma too, and has been working with one of the co-ops, shifting irrigation pipes. It's been great to have him around, swopping experiences and sharing some of the weight of being a foreigner in town. People welcome you – and hold you responsible – in every possible way. "Com he" and vigorous beckoning (actually this was in Masaya) ... I steel myself to stop assuming it's someone wanting dollars, soliciting a kiss and a cuddle, or a drunk after a fag, and I'm rewarded ... a school pupil practising English who wants to know what fruits grow in England, what the countryside's like, and wants to say he's going to have a technical career, even if it only begins after 2 years military service.

A 73 years old Tismeno passed me in the square and asked what I was going to do about his mango. He pulls a bird-eaten mango out of a bag and tells me the Cubans are bringing the country down (there are no Cubans in Tisma but there were a Cuban doctor and a Cuban teacher 3 or 4 years ago, and when I tell him I'm from England he takes it in his stride; England must be a town in Cuba). He's very pleasant about it, just doesn't know what's wrong with the birds that they should eat his mango. Later I hear that he took it to Celso, to complain that the Revolution hadn't stopped the birds eating his mango and what was Celso going to do about it. Expectations are very high in Nicaragua!

Tuesday 18th – I'm back in Masaya after another day in Tisma to take pictures of the nursery and records some songs of Celso and 'Andico el Tismeno', Tisma's most famous songster and the main carpenter of Tisma. He wants to know more about/from the Bradford Woodworkers co-op.

Harry had stayed in Tisma, and had been at the signing on ceremony for 100 Tismenos to join, no, to form, a sappers brigade – to learn how to lay explosives and land mines in case of a US invastion. Tisma is thought to be a possible landing place – isolated but close to Managua. I've hardly seen any military presence in Tisma. The only gun I've seen is Celso's AK47, Czech made, which he never takes out but would like some oil for.

Ana Maria

She's stuck in the house washing and cooking. She took me aside once and said, "You know, I'm very ill". "Ill with what?" "I'm ill in my heart. I'd like a change, just for a short time, something different. Maybe if there's a course to become a teacher I'd like to do it. I don't know that Celso would let me. Last year I did first grade (of secondary schooling). I didn't pay anything. Imagine! It wasn't like that before. It was only for those who had money. Do you see? Well, that's how it is".

Now her sister Nidia's here they share the load and it's easier. Yesterday Nidia went out and helped with the census for the new basic-foods distribution – a ration card that has each family's members and their ages – it will help streamline the existing system and apparently it's welcomed by just about everyone, as it signifies that the government is taking notice of their needs – this according to Nidia. Ana-Maria will help with the census too, maybe.

There are a hundred words to do with maize. Just on cold drinks, there are:

PINOLO – ground toasted corn with water;
POSOL – cooked pop-corn with water;
PINOLIO – pinolo with cocoa.

Rubbish

I have real difficulty knowing where to put it in Tisma. Anything edible goes on the floor for the pigs to clean up. A lot of other things seem to go on the floor too; for the women and children to clean up? Maria Lastenia lent me her teacher-training project which was partly a history of Tisma. She talks about burning rubbish as a recent innovation.

Religion

There are three churches in Tisma, none very influential. In one of the comarcas we visited, Las Cortezas, the Jehovah's Witnesses have been regularly visiting and saying that revolutionaries (i.e. anyone who is happy with the Revolution) are bad in the eyes of God and will suffer. Celso's answer: to visit Las Cortezas more often, explain what's going on in the country – the difficulties made by the US financed war, the social programmes they can benefit from – and to tell them that the Jehovah's Witnesses are not working in their interests. That's all, and having seen Celso in action it'll probably be enough to stop the JWs, who come from out of town, making political opposition out of peoples' genuine problems.

Most people here, in Nicaragua I mean, are firm Catholics. Don Francisco, in the Managua hospedaje: "Religion teaches you to bend your knees before making your demand. The Revolution teaches you to stand up straight before making your demands". "Are you and your family religious?" "But yes, of course, we're all religious here!"

Maria Lastenia is one of the most committed women I met in Tisma, very involved in education and very happy with the opportunities since 1979. Her husband is head teacher of the secondary school, Wilfredo Castro. The family is in the Nazarene evangelist church, and one of the daughters is actively involved in it. Another daughter married a Catholic church official: "No problem – we go to both churches now". "No problems with the Sandinistas?" "No, why should there be?"

Cardinal Obando, head of the Catholic hierarchy, is a problem, openly talking with the contras and making life very difficult for progressive catholic priests in Nicaragua. It is said that the only people persecuting the church in Nicaragua are the Catholic hierarchy themselves.

Rats

They seem to be mice in most houses, especially in the roofs; everyone in Tisma I've asked about the problem has looked at me strangely, as though I'd suggested they kill off their hens: "What problem?" However, the co-ops have rat poison and cartoon-pamphlets that tell the History of the Rat and also how to kill them, because the field-rats (mice?) eat crops. It seems the field mice and the town mice have a high sense of solidarity. The cartoon pamphlet on field mice control that Harry brought back from his co-op was found mutilated the next morning – chewed to bits by an offended house mouse.

More on Buses

I've been on quite a few now. I'm beginning to understand some of the problems. You'll remember that there are two doors, one at the front and one at the back, and every bus is full. The idea is that you get in at the front (paying 3 cordobas in Managua) and struggle down the aisle in time to get off the back at your stop. Timing is important. I've only seen one hefty woman with a box of tangerines on her head capable of moving from halfway down the bus to the back between two stops. I was forced out before my stop that time, and a couple of other casualties occurred – broken foot and crushed groin, nothing fatal.

Most people aim to get to the back well before their stop, but this creates the CLOT, which is difficult to get through; it often happens that you get empty standing space at the front while there's a CLOT of people crushed at the back for fear of missing their stop. Some passengers deal with the CLOT by staying up front and nipping off at their stop before passengers get on. However, if too many people do that you get big pressure up front too – this is the DOUBLE CLOT.

There's no real answer to the DOUBLE CLOT. One woman was bodily passed through a middle window when confronted with the DOUBLE CLOT, but this move is not generally advisable.

British Embassy

I called in for my cup of tea, filter cigarette, and a look at the Times and Guardian back copies up to about 10 days old. It seemed like the Westland stuff must have lifted the News programme ratings, among the hopeful left anyway! I guess it'll be over when I get back; I hope so – I don't like seeing people embarrassed. It didn't quite make cartoon status over here – agrarian reform, then Haiti, intervened. Richard Owen is the British Charge d'Affaires, pleasant and fairly well informed – though he didn't know Bradford was twinning with Tisma: "Oh, Bradford too!" he said.

He explained a little of the role of British and US multi-nationals here. British American Tobacco controls most of the cigarette making and distribution. Shell has about a third of petrol distribution. Nicaragua buys the oil, then Texaco and Esso refine it and, with others, distribute it. ICI sells fertilisers, more so since the US embargo (the embargo excludes trading within Nicaragua, so US firms can do internal distribution but not direct selling. They can also sell through, for example, Venezuelan or Costa Rican subsidiaries). ICI also does some bartering – fertiliser for cotton – but not much. UK government and UK companies won't trade any more than at present "because politics are such as they are". He's advised our Maggie that the Nicaraguan economy won't collapse, because there's nothing to collapse: it's more or less subsistence. He's clearly biding his time till the next post – doesn't seem to be very interested. Meanwhile I've got details of rum deals for Vinceremos Wines and Spirits, and I'll bring back a house sample.

I still haven't got March 10th confirmed from Aeroflot, maybe tomorrow before I give this letter to a group returning to Britain who have been picking coffee here.

I've been in fine health, except for losing weight – it doesn't take five minutes on a wooden chair before I get a sore bum. Harry reckons it's vitamins, or lack of them. So I'm eating more giant tangerines.

I'm getting my own feel for what's going on. Lots of movement but not much progress, almost entirely because the war takes up so many resources – 60% of the budget everyone says. So the international support makes a lot of difference – a few dollars can go a long way on social programmes that are waiting to go ahead except for lack of money. And isolating the US so the war can end would make a tremendous difference to what can go on.

Peter, one of the US volunteers, has just walked by with a box of "FACIAL TISSUE". I had thought that he was a computer scientist. He tells me it's his personal supply of facial tissue. I said I think he's fine without plastic surgery.

Ask me about hunting iguanas in Tisma.

I hope things are well in the University of Kentucky.

Your Brit in Tisma   *XXXXXXXXX*

PS. Aeroflot confirmed only to Moscow; on waiting list Moscow – London. If it's confirmed I'll be in London Tuesday 11th, I think 8pm, and I'll stay there for a few showers maybe, till Thursday 13th. Anyway I'll let someone know when/if it's confirmed.

PPS. For some reason the money hasn't come through for Tisma; now 9 days since I got the telegram saying John was sending it. I'll try ringing tonight.

xxxxx   19.2.86

Diary

Leon – Managua – Bluefields

Feb 18 – 28

Travel to Bluefields is slow getting started. A prerequisite is permission from the Migration Offices; it is needed for the Atlantic Coast where contra activity is widespread. The Migration Offices themselves need a letter of recommendation from a Nicaraguan organisation – in my case CNSP, the Comite Nicaraguense de Solidaridad con les Pueblos, the international solidarity organisation here. That achieved, plus photocopies of passport – 35 cords a side, not difficult to find commercially – Migration then need 2 to 3 days to process it, so I decided to get out of Managua and go north to Leon, a cotton town of some 100,000 population, where Peruvian Julia, who also came as a technical volunteer, is working on information systems for the Agrarian Reform Ministry, MIDINRA.

Inter-urban cars get up to Leon in 1½ hours after a 1 hour wait, for 300 cords. Leon is immediately lively, crowded and filthy. The walk from the Inter-urban to Hotel Europa is through the market and the train station. The market is open 7 days a week, and a cafe section stays open all night every night. Hotel Europa is luxurious, outside and inside, 900 cordobas with mosquitos and cockroaches included – nowhere eliminates those – and it serves a fine breakfast.

Julia's settled herself in – living in MIDINRA's Casa de Protocolo with Comandantes visiting every other day, and a driver on call day and night. She, or rather the driver, carried me off to a baseball match, Leon v Granada. The old political rivalry between the two towns dates back centuries, but it isn't reflected in baseball; Leon, the champions, won easily in a match that everyone assessed as boring. It was packed, maybe ten thousand people, and serviced by dozens of sellers of all ages, pushing fresco, beer, tortilla and grilled beef, peanuts, banana chips, oranges and cigarettes.

Next day, Thursday, was my only day in Leon. I made contact with University teachers on the first Statistics degree in Nicaragua – producing its first graduates in 1986. This is the first committed group of professionals I've met, and will benefit from anything the Radical Statistics Group in Britain can do – second-hand statistics books, calculators, or visiting lecturers. They have seven or eight calculators on the statistics degree course, between 8 lecturers and 80 or so students. Later, Julia showed me a MIDINRA questionnaire on idle land, full of ambiguities and design faults. I'd love to do that kind of survey work here.

Back early Friday to Managua, straight to a 3 hour queue for bus and boat tickets to Bluefields. Most of the people in the queue were from the Atlantic Coast itself, going home or visiting relatives. Many are from Miskito and English-speaking Afro-Nicaraguan communities. Suddenly it felt like I was among foreigners, themselves unsure and maybe suspicious in Managua, and also suspicious of why I was going to Bluefields. English spoken! All this is too much like going home. The ticket costs 430 cordobas all the way – a 5 hour bus ride to El Rama, and 5 more hours by boat to Bluefields, over the mountainous interior and down to the Caribbean coast. That compares with 2000 cordobas to go by taxi from the Hospedaje San Juan to the bus terminal in Managua at 3am Saturday morning.

The bus leaves at 4.30; I have a seat!

The Trip Out to Bluefields

The bus has a 'motorway stop' for breakfast (the usual beans & rice & meat & tortilla & salad. Yes, for breakfast!) and huge 2 kilo blocks of local cheese sold to every other passenger. The road stops at El Rama, already on the other side of Nicaragua's North-South mountain range. There the bus stops, turns round, and goes back to Managua. The only road connecting the Pacific and Atlantic sides of the country was built in the North since the Revolution, but it's been made impassable to civilian traffic by the contras.

So if you decide not to take the unreliable plane which suffers from the US trade embargo on spare parts, you get the bus to El Rama, and then a 5 hour boat journey on the ironically named 'Bluefields Express' down El Rio Escondido, 'the hidden river'.

The 'Express' takes 60-100 people, cramped but not uncomfortable, on its daily journey. Soldiers on top in case of contra attack – one launch was destroyed in 1985. With a name like 'the hidden river', I had expected a romantic voyage. But El Rio Escondido was not narrow with overhanging tropical forest; parrots did not screech overhead; there were no rapids and no crocodiles, and very little colour apart from green. Rather boring, and only emphasising the difference between the atlantic coast region and the rest of the country.

Mix on boat is ⅔ mestizo, ⅓ creole, reflecting Bluefield's demography, according to its paper Sunrise, and the Encuentro edition on 'The Coast', in which I immerse myself on the way down. A quick lesson in racial/cultural communities here. Mestizo: Spanish-speaking indigenous Indian and European mixed heritage, common throughout Nicaragua. Miskito, Rama, and Sumu: indigenous Indian communities, almost exclusively in the Atlantic Coast region. Creole, or Afro-Nicaraguan: English-speaking communities with origins in Britain's rule over the Atlantic coast, and its slave-holdings. Garifonas: a small mixed Carib Indian and Afro-Nicaraguan community.

Arrival and Accommodation in Bluefields

Leon (Remember? the baseball champions) are in town for a match with the Coast team – attracting a crowd from other towns. Result: no accommodation except for the floor of a run-down, waterless hotel. It turns out that all the hotels are like that. But I found Hospedaje Santa Rosa, just beyond the bridge, in an idyllic setting by the river with breezy rooms. To be recommended especially in the rainy season, when there's water.

Political Mood

In Bluefields it is totally different from the Pacific region. Everyone, except the officials and one acquaintance from the street, was generally negative about life in general. This is what I had been led to believe by my reading on the way down.

The coast has a history separate from the rest of Nicaragua; controlled by British traders and colonialists in the 18th and 19th centuries, the Miskito kingdom was more an English-inspired defence against the Spanish than a means of representing community needs. The British brought slaves who stayed longer than their owners, who were replaced at the beginning of this century by US marines and fruit companies.

The US presence declined from the forties, and the whole Atlantic coast was neglected from then on. Although migration from the Pacific side means that the majority of the population is Spanish-speaking mestizo, it is a small majority, and the most rooted populations culturally are the Miskito Indians and the black creoles.

Many people are trilingual in Miskito, English and Spanish; and some others speak Sumu, Rama, or Garifona, the minority Indian languages. So the area is culturally different, is anti-Spanish historically, and looks back to the 'good old days' when the US companies were thriving.

The Atlantic Coast is the name for the whole region to the east of the central mountain range, with half the land mass but just one tenth of the population of Nicaragua. It was untouched by the liberation struggle, so it has none of the pride and awareness of the Pacific. Nonetheless, it suffers all the hardships of economic privation and dislocation that the contras' war imposes on all of Nicaragua and, in addition, a history of manipulation and severe exploitation.

That's a recipe for resentment and confusion which the FSLN took until 1983-4 to understand. Up to then, some of the FSLN's workers who went to the coast from the pacific were a little resentful that the Coast's people failed to receive the Revolution and its ringing slogans with joy and extreme gratitude. From 1981, some Miskito leaders joined the contras and played on the confusion to turn a messy situation into one dangerous for the Revolution as a whole – they urged Miskitos to take up arms against the 'foreign communists'. The assessment of Miskito leaders who did not join the contras is that those who did so were attracted by the dollars to be gained. (Dollars have more importance in Nicaragua than even before the Revolution?!)

The result was that the army had to go in strongly to ensure Nicaragua's north-east border, where it was quite possible a contra/Miskito controlled area could declare a parallel government and call in foreign assistance. To the vast majority of Miskitos, these developments were going on above their heads, but they saw a Spanish-speaking army (which was not 'their own' as it is perceived on the Pacific) shooting it out with Miskitos, and in the process abruptly and without consultation shifting border villages' inhabitants to locations away from the fighting. Serious stuff!

Several things have changed since then. Those of the Miskito contras who have refused dialogue with the government have turned to terrorism and disruption of social projects – for instance, late last year, one of the two river launches used by the bilingual education project was destroyed. This is awful, and it helps the Miskito population to understand what is going on. some Miskito contras have dialogued with the government – those who are less interested in dollars than in their communities – and many have laid down arms and returned.

The government has put a lot of investment into the coast, so that schools and clinics and employment are beginning to show that the 'foreign' Managua government does have something to offer. And, more important than anything else, there's the Autonomy Project. Formally this will mean autonomous government on the coast, including economic autonomy, within the Nicaraguan constitution. Politically, it is the means by which the coast people will determine what their aspirations are and how they will resolve them. All government offices are to be headed by coast people, and the door-to-door consultation on the project is already providing a better expression of problems and political mood than there has ever been before.

So Maribel, living next door to my idyllic hospedaje, of Miskito mother and black father, says: "The government isn't giving us peace, but neither are the people in the bush. We don't want Reagan to give money because that will keep the fighting going. Autonomy? That's good, if it comes".

I had the tastiest lobster of my life in Bluefields, three times. I spent one night in a reggae night-club. And one night, past the Bingo Hall, past a cake shop (at last, a cake shop!), Lambeth struck. Field Marshal Michael Archangel, front-line poet from Brixton, London, reciting on Bluefields streets. I was totally taken by surprise. He outdid even the Pacific Nicaraguans in friendliness and self-pride, talking and reciting non-stop. He claimed to be on a cultural exchange from Lambeth, though he didn't know who he was to be exchanged with. I guess that Bluefields will be intrigued by him. I asked "Where are you staying here?" Michael Archangel said "On the frontline, man". And I never saw him again.

I arrived on Saturday night, and on Monday was back to investigating – this time with the thought that Caribbean Labour Solidarity, the London-based organisation that gives tremendous support to Caribbean workers' groups, should extend its work to include the Atlantic coast of Nicaragua. I talked to an FSLN worker, to CIDCA (the Centre for Investigation and Documentation of the Atlantic Coast), and to regional trade union official Jose Chan. All born on the coast, and all very committed and capable.

In the Bluefields region (about 500,000 people, about a quarter of the coast), campesino agriculture is not as important as are bigger companies – for prawn fishing and processing, sugar, African palm for cooking oil, boat building and repair. All are state-owned – they were originally either Somoza-owned or foreign-owned (mainly US, one by Cuban gusanos), but they refused to invest after the Revolution, and so were taken over.

It seems that these wage-labourers are the source of most advanced thinking here, comparable to the co-ops in Tisma, for example. Adult education is big. I visited a plant on El Bluff and many of the fishing-industry workers were about to spend the closed season (when prawns are spawning) in school, all paid for. Workers in the factories have priority in the distribution of clothes: there's a CAT (Centro de Abastecimiento de los Trabajadores) in Bluefields, where workers go on an allotted day to get a quota of clothes and other goods at low prices. The productive workers are allotted days at the beginning of the month – so they get first pick of the goods that come in on the first of each month.

Bluefields has no sewage system and not a lot of deep latrines. Houses on the rivers have overhanging 'toilets'.

Houses not on the rivers contribute to sewage runs that often reach the streets instead of the rivers.

One poster reads "Forward Ever" – so Grenada lives! Although many of the black population have temporary origins in St Vincent, Jamaica and other Caribbean islands, current links are almost non-existent: emigration from the coast this century was to the US, the Cayman Islands, San Adres (Colombia) and Managua. Reestablishing those Caribbean links is an important part of the Autonomy Project on the Atlantic Coast.

And so, back to Managua via bus and boat again, after 4 days in Bluefields.

Via Crucis Arrives in Managua

Via Crucis (March of the Cross), a Catholic protest march more than 200 km from Jalapa near the Honduran border to Managua, inspired and led by Foreign Minister Padre Miguel D'Escoto, calling for peace, and for unity among catholics. Miguel D'Escoto is the same priest who went on hunger strike against US aid for the contras last summer, and has always sought peaceful ways of ending the contra war.

The entry of the Via Crucis to Victory Square was reminiscent of a few other marches I've been on – lots of banners and posters, lots of meeting of old friends, a disabled contingent leading the way: contra victims.

The final act of the march wasn't reminiscent of any march I've been on. It was an open-air catholic mass, presided over by 30 priests, interspersed with contributions from marchers. It was dark when the act started, but slow-burning sticks were distributed and lit, giving a candle-lit church atmosphere. Among the contributors was a 12-year-old marcher – he was introduced as an adult education organiser from Ocotal!!

Everyone was waiting for D'Escoto's contribution. It was worth waiting for. Very eloquently, he verbally ripped the clothes off Cardenal Obando's back, showed them to be foreign-owned, and challenged him to find some Nicaraguan ones. Obando is the Pope-appointed head of the Nicaraguan Catholic Church, who has refused to condemn the contra atrocities and has made an infamous visit to the USA which will have helped Reagan's $100m attempts to feed these same contras, meanwhile calling on Nicaragua to negotiate with them.

Obando has quite ruthlessly ignored the terrible efects on all Nicaraguan people of the contras' work, and ignored too the fact that they would not exist but for foreign (US) finance – a fact admitted by everyone else, including the US government itself. Miguel D'Escoto laid it on the line for him. He said it was not the role of a leader of the Nicaraguan church to sell his country to the USA. That Obando and the church hierarchy no longer spoke for God in Nicaragua, that Obando should think twice before leaving the country again and that his role was to talk to Nicaraguans. That the Nicaraguan people, though not perfect, could be compared to Jesus who also had to face up to the anger of an empire because of His search for a just way of living.

I'm sure that this is a new phase of church-state relations in Nicaragua, which up to now have been marked by continuous efforts by the government to allow the church hierarchy space to act within the terms of national integrity, even if in opposition to the government. Now that Obando seems to have given up all idea of respecting national integrity, this Via Crucis march, and presumably future events, will educate catholics – 95% of the population – to the fact that the church hierarchy does not represent the wishes of the people or of God in Nicaragua. However necessary, that is a difficult path to take, since over half

Nicaragua's priests are foreign and the structure of the church is such that all appointments and indeed all actions of priests (progressive or not) are sanctioned (or not) by the hierarchy.

Sunday 2nd March was memorable for a send-off for the second British coffee-picking brigade, which was returning to Britain the next day. It was fantastic to see a bright Nicaragua Solidarity Campaign banner behind a Nicaraguan folk group playing to a British audience – but in Nicaragua! And of course, it's much cheaper to have the group play in Nicaragua.

Back to Tisma for my last four days, bringing TecNICA organiser Shelley Sherman for an overnight stay, her first holiday in five months. For once no need for her to worry about a group being late for meetings; no placating irate volunteers whose expectations (of work) didn't live up to what they found. She loved it and so the Tisma Project has a sympathiser in Managua, eager for excuses to get out to Tisma again.

We stayed with Celso and Ana-Maria again. Ana's sister Nidia is planning to stay permanently and build a smaller house on the ground where Celso and Ana-Maria's old shack stood. Her husband Juan is conductor on the new bus, which Nidia proclaims is just as well, because the wage he brings in is all she gets from him! Ana-Maria is voluntary treasurer for the bus, looking after the takings and keeping the books. I swopped four 500 cordoba bills for the equivalent in 50 cordoba notes from the bus takings – the 50 cordoba notes have FSLN founder Carlos Fonseca on one side, the entry of the FSLN into Managua in July 1979 on the other, and a Sandino watermark. Costing 5 pence a note, we can surely sell or auction them at £5 each in Bradford ...

Chess

On Saturday afternoon, I came across two 10-year-old boys playing chess in the street, sat and watched, and then played. At last I've found a skill I can teach! Next time ("next time", I'm already talking in those terms; when, 1988, after my temporary Sheffield job finishes?), I'll bring half-a-dozen sets and start a chess school. Maybe the Casa de Cultura will be built by then.

Farewell Party

Saturday night, I invited everyone who was involved in the future projects and everyone who had been especially helpful. We had a cake with 'Bradford – Tisma – Peace' written on it, made by a Tisma woman for 3000 cordobas. A fresco with sugar and oranges donated from Manuel's shop. A box of salt crackers that I'd nipped into Managua for on Friday, and four water melons donated by the Lilliam Velasquez co-op. And some rum. It was billed for 5pm, and that sorted out the time-keepers: by 6 o'clock only Jairo, one of the school pupils, and Juanita, the librarian, and her husband, had arrived.

Cold start, but hot finish. Andico arrived with his new guitar (45,000 cords, part donated by the FSLN in Masaya in recognition of Andico's long service of song-writing and generally being a likeable person), and also brought a friend from outside Tisma who had a guitar. Here's the list of guests who arrived. They represent very well the Tisma Project link in Tisma itself: Jairo Selva Sotelo, a 15-year-old school student with polio affecting one leg – singer and artist; Teresa Selva M, 15-year old school student, Jairo's neighbour; Wilfredo Castro, the Principal of Lilliam Velasquez Secondary School; Maria Lastenia, the Principal of the Pio-Pio Nursery School; William Membreno, the dentist, and responsible for the Health Clinic; Juanita Miranda, the Librarian, and the only English-speaker; Ana-Maria Olivas, Nidia Olivas, & Celso Chavarria, the Mayor and family; Jose Sotelo, the Treasurer of Lilliam Velasquez co-op, and President of Tisma's Comite Comarcal, the town council; 3 others from the co-operative, including its President, a 50-year old who had just returned from coffee-picking and who with Jose quizzed me on workers' organisation in Britain; Manuel Gutierrez, Kath's good friend, shop-owner and the Water Authority in Tisma.

And so to leaving

Leaving Tisma on Sunday, on the council bus, packed solid with at least 40 people in a 21-seater, I cursed having finished my seventh and last slide film without getting a picture of the grain store, built in the last couple of years and painted in big letters *"ENABAS: ALMACEN POPULAR, TISMA"*. I waved goodbye to Jairo's mother who was visiting relatives in one of the comarcas, and settled down to sweat it out, crouched on the floor holding someone's bag of tomatoes to prevent them getting crushed.

A final Tisma gift was a lift in the bus to the door of the TecNICA hospedaje – the bus had an hour's turn-round time in Managua, and the driver will be ever remembered for his generosity in saving me two Managua bus-rides on my last day. After 2½ months and so many friendships begun, it's been a wrench to leave. All the TecNICA people – Shelley, Barbara, Geoff, Ed and Mirna, were there to see me off; long may their embraces last.

Back in London, 11th March

So many traffic jams – I didn't realise what a demand it was to ask to be picked up at Heathrow. So many tall, tall buildings, street after street of them, like a different planet. I knew that the people rushing on the pavement didn't have the time to talk to each other, let alone know what their problems were and work to solve them.

No-one was speaking Spanish, but it isn't just that: the enormous adverts that I never usually notice seemed grabbing, far from rational, and out of control. Newspaper headlines didn't seem to make sense, as I'd begun to expect them to: *"LIFE THREE TIMES OVER"* was one – and I thought maybe someone had discovered a long-life diet, but it was lurid details of a rapist given three life sentences.

I've been subjected to two and a half months of taking life seriously, and now everybody seemed to be saying "Don't take life seriously, it's not worth it".

Back in Bradford, the real work begins: bringing Nicaragua alive for those who haven't yet visited it. Perhaps it *is* worth taking life seriously.

Thanks Nicaragua,
Steve

Author's note:–
This publication would not have been possible without the encouragement and practical support of Graham Walker, Roland Rance, and the Bradford Resource Centre.

These organisations will send you information about Nicaragua on request:

The Nicaragua Solidarity Campaign, 23 Bevenden Street, London N1 6BH. Telephone: 01-608 0414

Oxfam, 274 Banbury Road, Oxford OX2 7DZ

War On Want, 1 London Bridge Street, London SE1

The Tisma Project (Bradford – Tisma community twinning), c/o Bradford Resource Centre, 31 Manor Row, Bradford BD1 4PS